Praise for *ABCs of Oystering on the Chesapeake Bay*

"As a lifelong outdoorsman and steward of the Chesapeake Bay, I've learned that the best guides are the ones that teach you to see the water with both curiosity and respect. Susan Swift's *ABCs of Oystering on the Chesapeake Bay* does just that. It wonderfully details the work of watermen during the harvesting of oysters and presents the life on the docks with clarity, humility, and a genuine love for the Bay. It's an accessible, eye-opening introduction to the industry—engaging for newcomers and enough depth for seasoned readers who want to refresh their understanding of sustainable oystering. This book captures the pulse of the shoreline and the craft of oystering in a way that invites you to learn, celebrate, and protect this iconic watershed. It's a thoughtful tribute to the people who work the water and a compelling reminder of our duty to protect the Bay."

—Congressman Rob Wittman (VA- 01)

"Susan Swift and Heather Cockrell have done it again! The *ABCs of Oystering on the Chesapeake Bay* is as beautiful and informative as their first book, The *ABCs of Crabbing*. As a board member of the Virginia Oyster Trail, I am certainly an advocate for oysters. I know children and parents alike will learn something new about everyone's favorite mollusk in this clever ABC book; I sure did. I hope this book finds its way up and down the Virginia Oyster Trail and beyond."

—Shauna McCranie, Executive Director,
Reedville Fishermen's Museum

"From the very first page, the vivid illustrations capture the reader's attention and continue to engage throughout the book. Through thoughtful and creative writing, the story offers a window into the world of oysters and the hardworking watermen who harvest them. For readers seeking a book that is both educational and captivating, this one delivers from start to finish."

—Monica Schenemann, Virginia Waterwoman Secretary,
Virginia Waterman's Association Board Member,
Virginia Marine Products Board

"The *ABCs of Oystering on the Chesapeake Bay* is more than a beautifully illustrated children's book, it's a creative tool for teaching the next generation about the importance of protecting our natural resources and preserving the watermen's way of life. Young readers will get a glimpse of the Bay's ecology, and the career paths it sustains by fostering curiosity, stewardship, and pride in the Chesapeake Bay region. Thank you, Mrs. Swift, for continuing to highlight some of our most treasured resources."

—Delegate Hillary Pugh Kent,
Virginia House of Delegates, District 67

ABCs

OF OYSTERING
ON THE CHESAPEAKE BAY

By
Susan Swift

Illustrations By
Heather Cockrell

BELLE ISLE BOOKS
www.belleislebooks.com

ISBN (Paperback): 978-1-966369-00-4
ISBN (Hardcover): 978-1-966369-01-1
Library of Congress Control Number: 2025921590

Designed by Sami Langston
Production managed by Sydney Wright

Published by
Belle Isle Books (an imprint of Brandylane Publishers, Inc.)
5 S. 1st Street
Richmond, Virginia 23219

BELLE ISLE BOOKS
www.belleislebooks.com

belleislebooks.com | brandylanepublishers.com

This book is dedicated to all the commercial watermen on the Chesapeake Bay, especially my favorite watermen, Keith and Zach, as well as to Macy, who encourages me to dream big!

Did you know oysters have been around for millions of years? Scientists have found 150 million-year-old oyster fossils, which means they lived on the Earth when dinosaurs were still alive.

Oysters are incredibly helpful to the environment of the Chesapeake Bay and have been caught and eaten by natives, settlers, and us for thousands of years, or more! The Algonquin Native American word for **Chesapeake** is *Chesepiooc*. Some interpretations of the word translate to 'great shellfish bay,' which the Bay certainly is! The Chesapeake Bay is a great habitat for oysters because it is a mix of freshwater and saltwater. All of the oysters in the Bay are called Eastern Oysters.

The Chesapeake Bay is the biggest *estuary* in the United States. An estuary is a mix of fresh and saltwater. This *brackish water* is exactly the type of water oysters need. The Chesapeake Bay is bordered by the states of Maryland and Virginia. It covers 4,480 square miles and is 200 miles long.

Let's learn about how these amazing creatures live and how they are caught for us to enjoy.

A is for AQUACULTURE

Aquaculture is one way that oysters are raised and harvested in the Chesapeake Bay. The baby oysters are put into cages, which can float on the top, sit on the bottom, or can be anchored in columns in the water. These are called *oyster farms.*

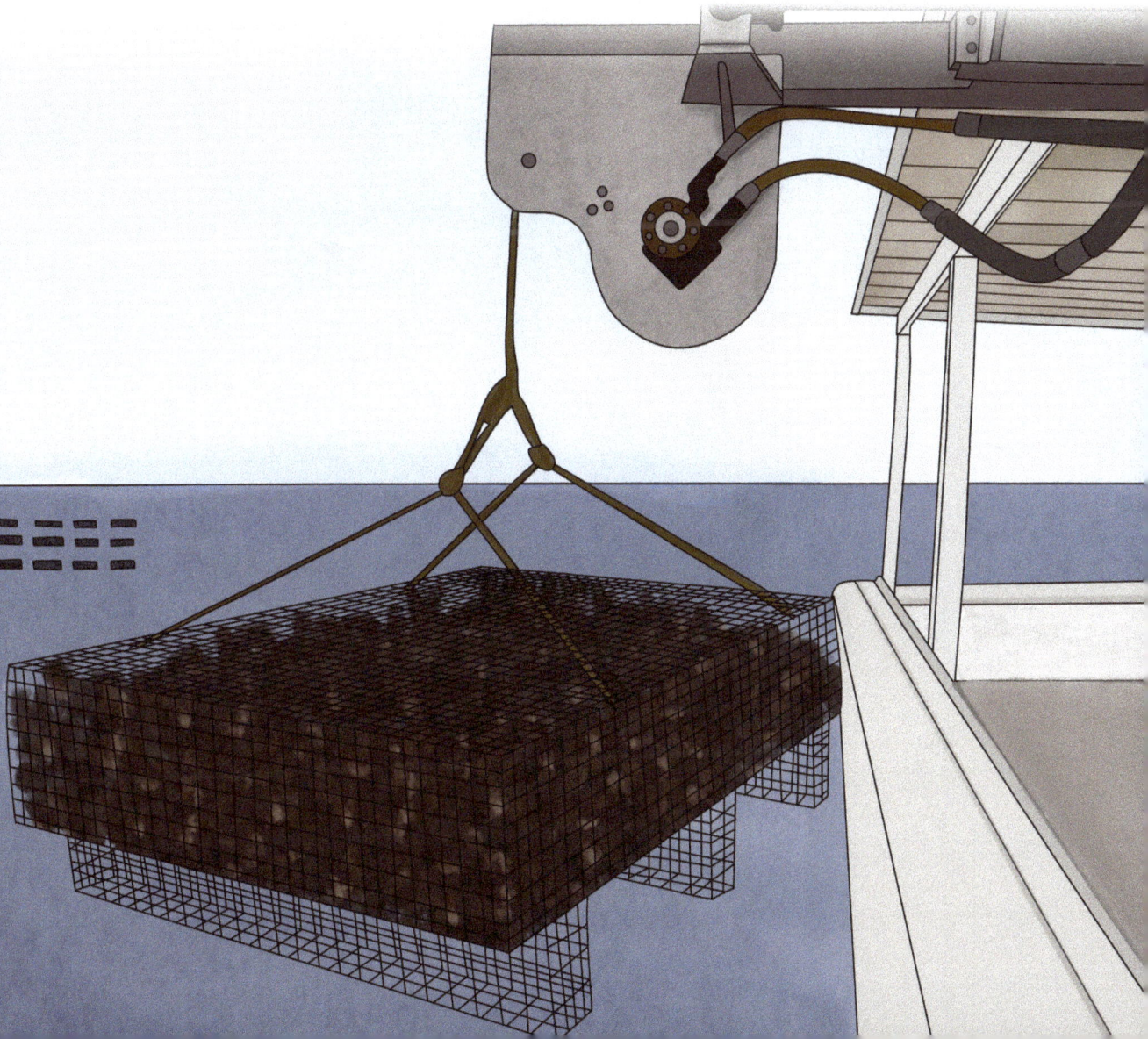

B is for BIVALVE

Oysters are *bivalve* shellfish, which means they have two shells attached to one end with a hinge, so that they can open and close. Their soft bodies are in the middle of the two shells.

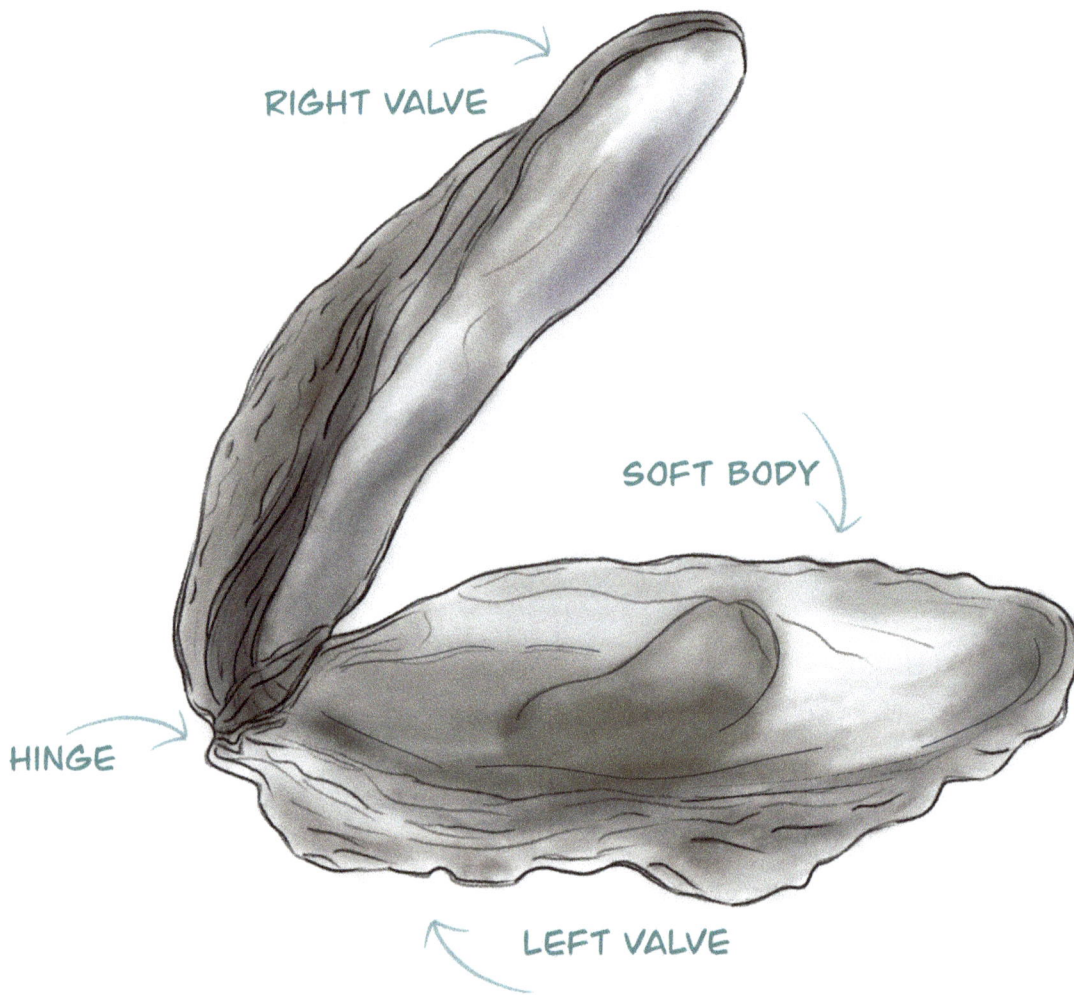

RIGHT VALVE

SOFT BODY

HINGE

LEFT VALVE

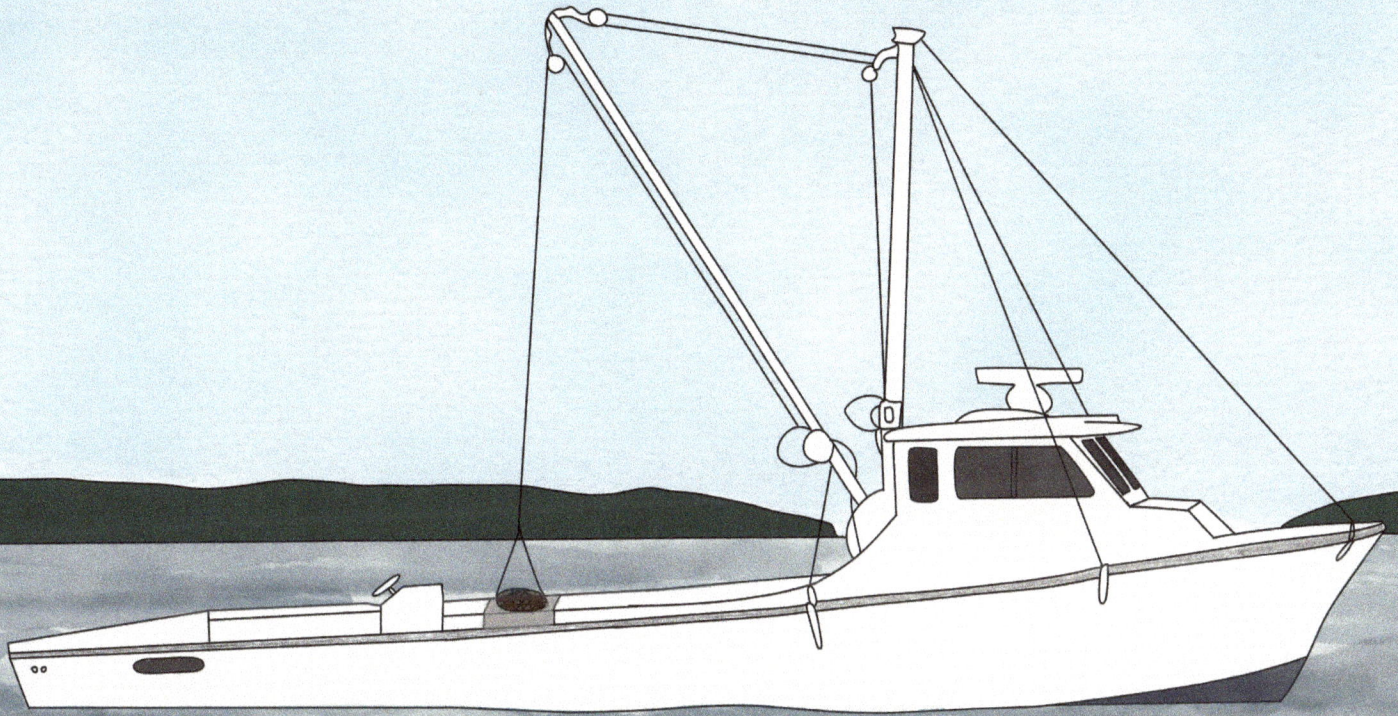

C is for CHESAPEAKE BAY DEADRISE

The *Chesapeake Bay Deadrise* boat is the traditional work boat used by watermen in the Chesapeake Bay. This is the most common type of boat used by oystermen because they have large, open backs that can store the oysters as they are brought onto the boat. Some oystermen use skiffs, which are open, flat-bottom boats.

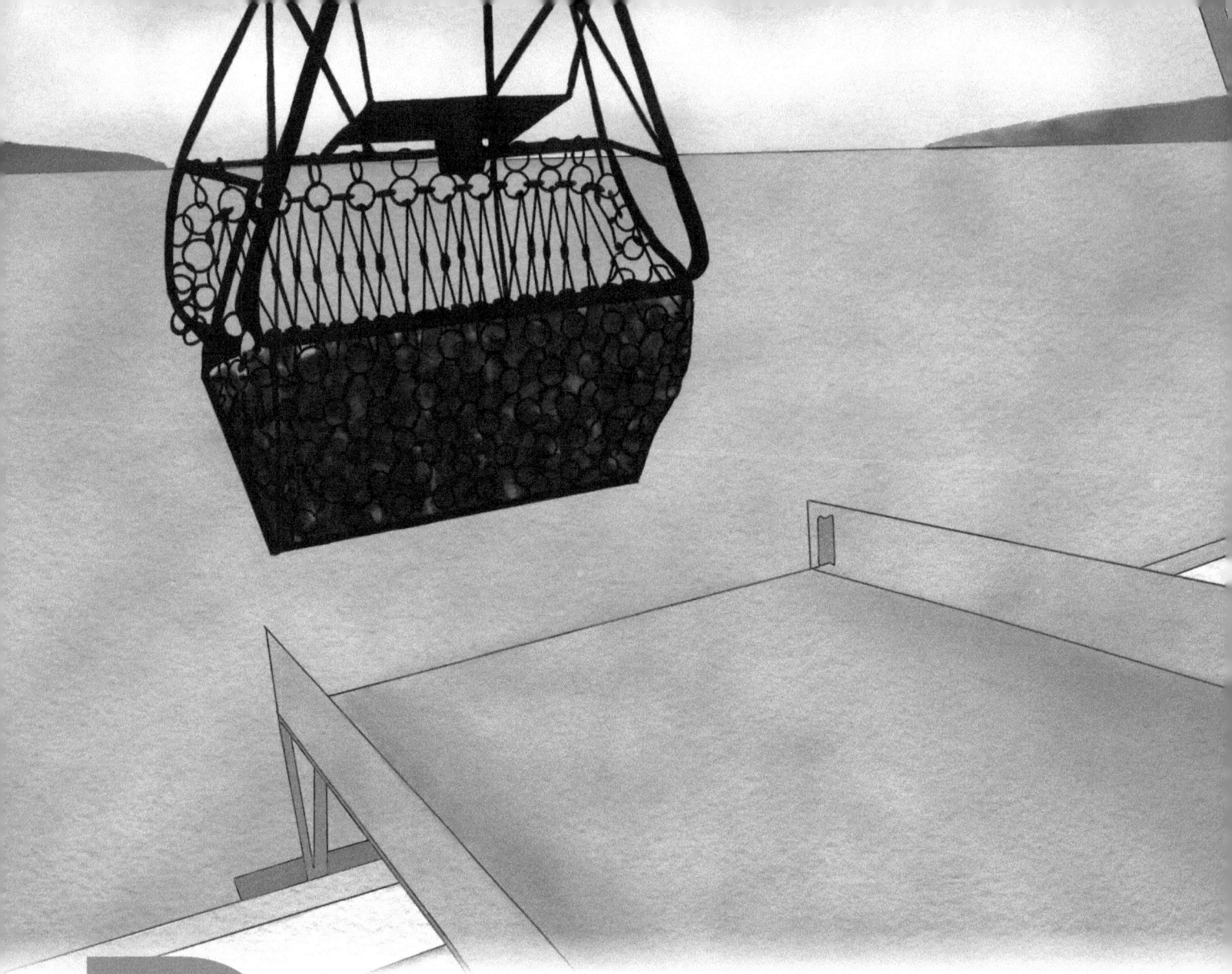

D is for DREDGE

Oystermen harvest oysters using an *oyster dredge*. A dredge is a metal frame with a chain bag. The dredge is slowly pulled along the bottom, collecting oysters, then brought up to the surface with a motorized winder, or long ago, pulled by hand.

E is for ECOSYSTEM

Oysters are an important part of the Chesapeake Bay's *ecosystem*, a community of animals and plants that live together. They are part of the food chain: Oysters eat algae, and are eaten by crabs, fish, birds, otters, raccoons, other small animals, and us!

F is for FILTER FEEDERS

Oysters are *filter feeders*. They pull water through their bodies, filtering food to eat. They also filter out things which are harmful to their ecosystem: nitrogen, phosphorus, and carbon. This leaves the water cleaner and clearer. A single adult oyster can clean up to 50 gallons of water a day!

Clean

Dirty

G is for GROW

Baby oysters, called *spat*, attach themselves to other oysters in order to grow. After a few months, the spat are called *seed* oysters. Oysters are full-grown and harvested when they are between one and a half to three years old.

H is for HARVEST

Oystermen *harvest*, or collect, oysters. When oysters are harvested, they are sorted by size. Oystermen call long, thin oysters "snaps". Sometimes, oystermen find oyster shells that have **no** live oyster inside. They are called "*cluckers*"!

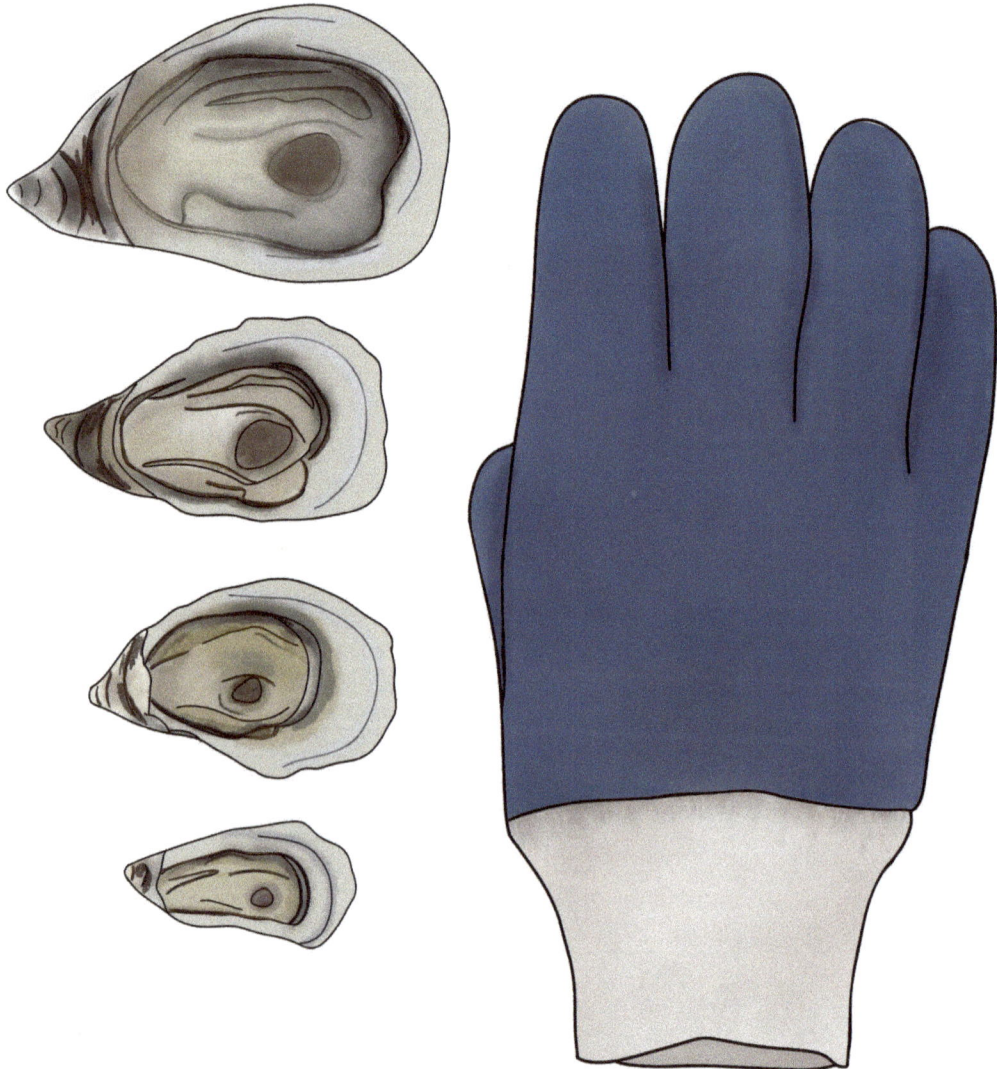

I is for INTO BUSHEL BASKETS

When oystermen collect the oysters, they put them *into bushel baskets.* Bushel baskets are strong wooden or plastic baskets. Oystermen measure how many oysters they harvest by counting the bushel baskets.

J is for JEOPARDY

Many people, including oystermen, work very hard to make sure nothing puts oysters in *jeopardy*, or in danger. Oysters can get diseases called *Dermo* and *MSX*, water pollution can kill them, and overharvesting can make the oyster population smaller.

K is for KEEP

Oysters must be 3 inches long to *keep*. Oystermen measure the oysters they catch on a cull table. Small oysters are thrown back into the water so they can continue growing.

L is for LIMIT

Oystermen have a *limit* on how many bushels of oysters can be collected each day, depending on where and when they are harvested. This prevents them from being overharvested.

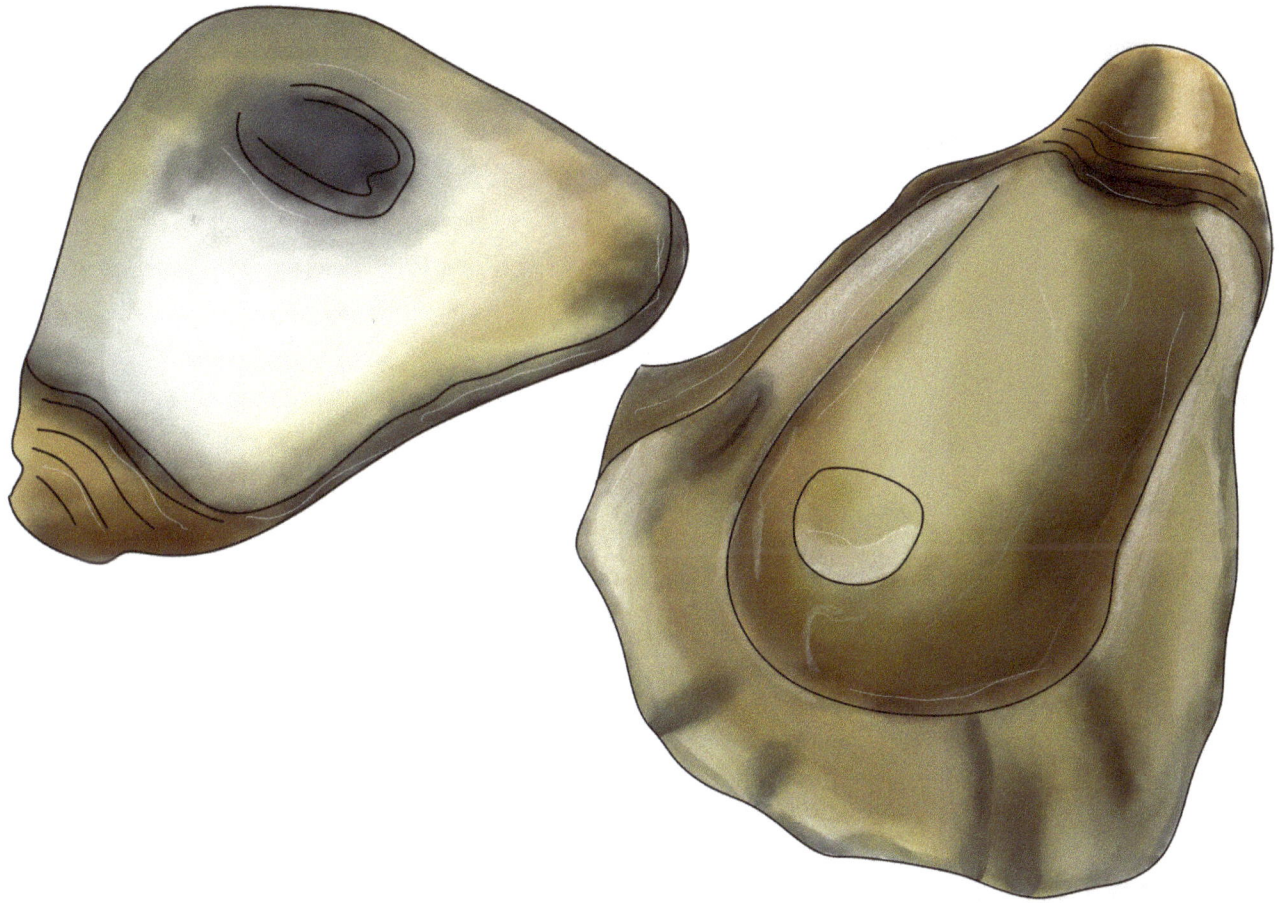

M is for MOLLUSK

An oyster is a type of animal called a *mollusk*. Mollusks are invertebrates, which means they have no backbone. Their shells protect their soft bodies. Clams, mussels, and scallops are mollusks, too.

N is for NATIVE AMERICANS

The *Native Americans* who lived along the coasts of the Chesapeake Bay used oysters for thousands of years before European settlers arrived. They collected and ate oysters throughout the year. Oyster shells were also used to make tools, weapons, and jewelry.

is for OYSTERMEN

Women and men who harvest oysters to sell are called oystermen. Oystermen work very hard collecting oysters from October until March.

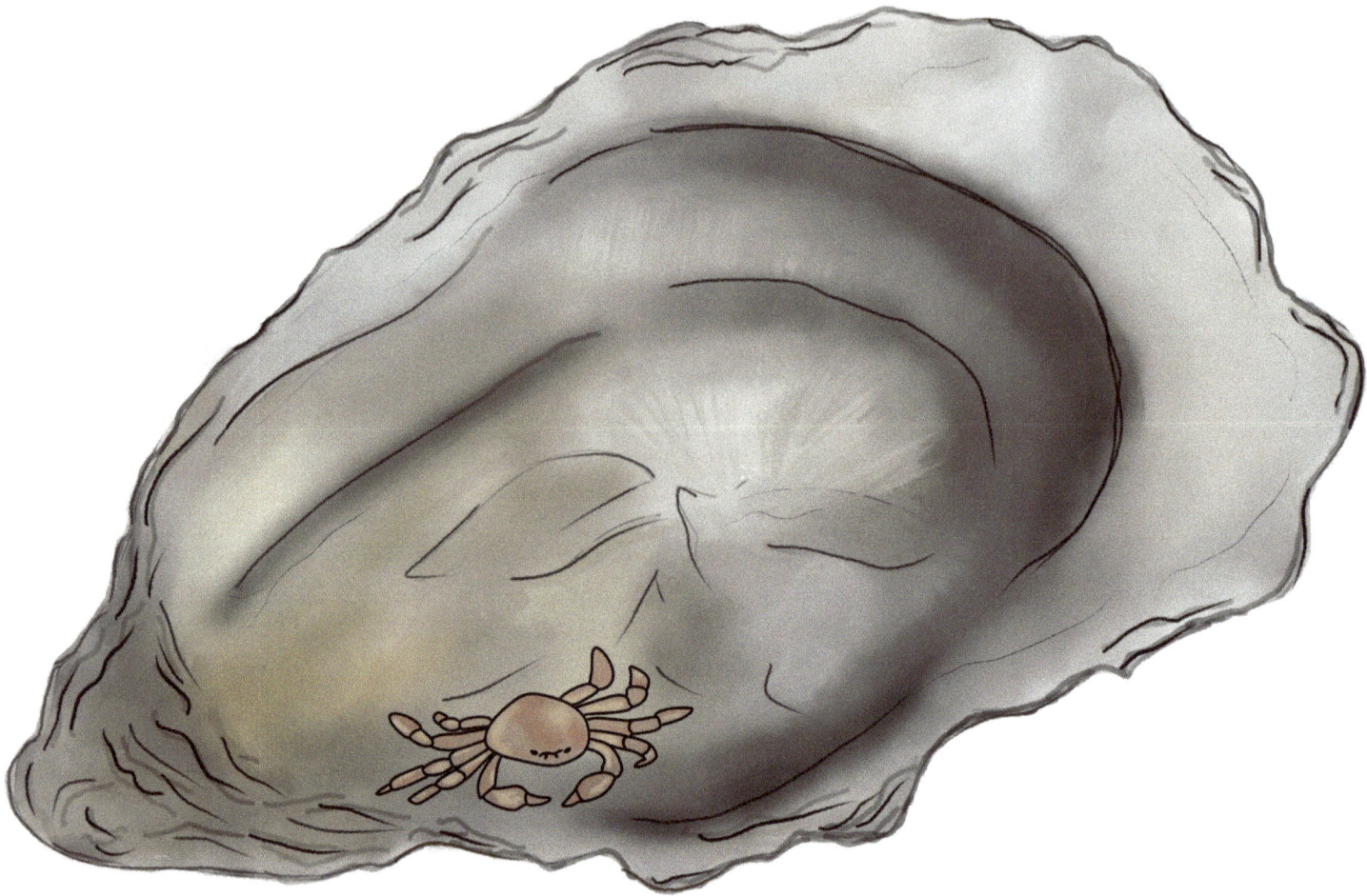

P is for PEA CRAB

You may find a small crab inside of an oyster. They are called pea crabs, which may live inside an oyster for their whole life. A pea crab gets food from the oyster and can be eaten with the oyster. It is considered good luck to find and eat a pea crab!

Q is for AQUATIC HABITAT

Oysters live and grow in aquatic habitats, or underwater. Because they filter the water for food, they must be in moving, or flowing water to survive.

SUBMERGED
ROCKS
DANGER
OYSTER
REEF

R is for REEF

Wild oysters grow on oyster beds, or reefs. Reefs are large groups of oysters that grow on top of each other. As more and more oysters attach to older oysters, oyster reefs grow in size. Oyster reefs often provide shelter for fish, crabs, shrimp, and other sea animals. Oystermen call the reefs "oyster rocks."

S is for SHUCK

To eat an oyster, it must be opened, or shucked. To shuck the oyster, the shell is pried open with an oyster knife and the meat is taken out from the inside.

T is for TONGING

Tonging is another way that oysters are harvested. *Hand tonging* is gathering oysters from the bottom with two long-handled rakes that open and close like scissors and pulling them up by hand. In *patent tonging*, the rakes are opened, closed, and raised by a motor.

U is for USE

Every part of the oyster can be used. First, we eat them! Raw oysters, roasted oysters, fried oysters, oyster chowder, and oyster stew are just a few ways that people eat oysters. Second, empty oyster shells can be recycled and put back into the water on existing oyster reefs, or in piles to create new reefs. This gives baby oysters a place to grow.

V is for VEGETARIAN

Oysters are vegetarians. They eat algae, which are tiny green plants in the water. Oysters have gills like fish, which they use to filter out the algae to eat. This is helpful to their ecosystem because algae can block light from other plants and animals living in the water.

Micro Algae

W

is for WINDER

A *winder* is used to bring oysters onto the boat during dredging or tonging. It is powered by a hydraulic motor.

X is for EXTRA IMPORTANT

Oysters are eXtra important to the bay: They provide food for fish, crabs, other sea animals, and us! They are *filter feeders*, removing algae, nitrogen, and phosphorus from the water. Finally, oyster beds provide a habitat for new oysters and shelter for small fish, crabs, shrimp, and other sea creatures.

Y is for YEAR

An oyster grows an inch each year. How do we know how old they are? Oysters grow rings on their shells each year, like a tree! Oysters can live up to 30 years in the wild.

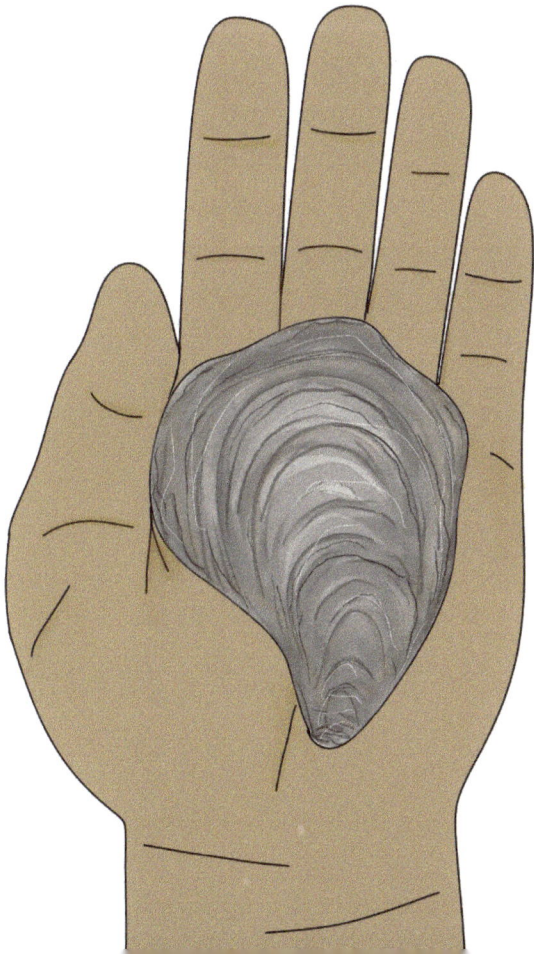

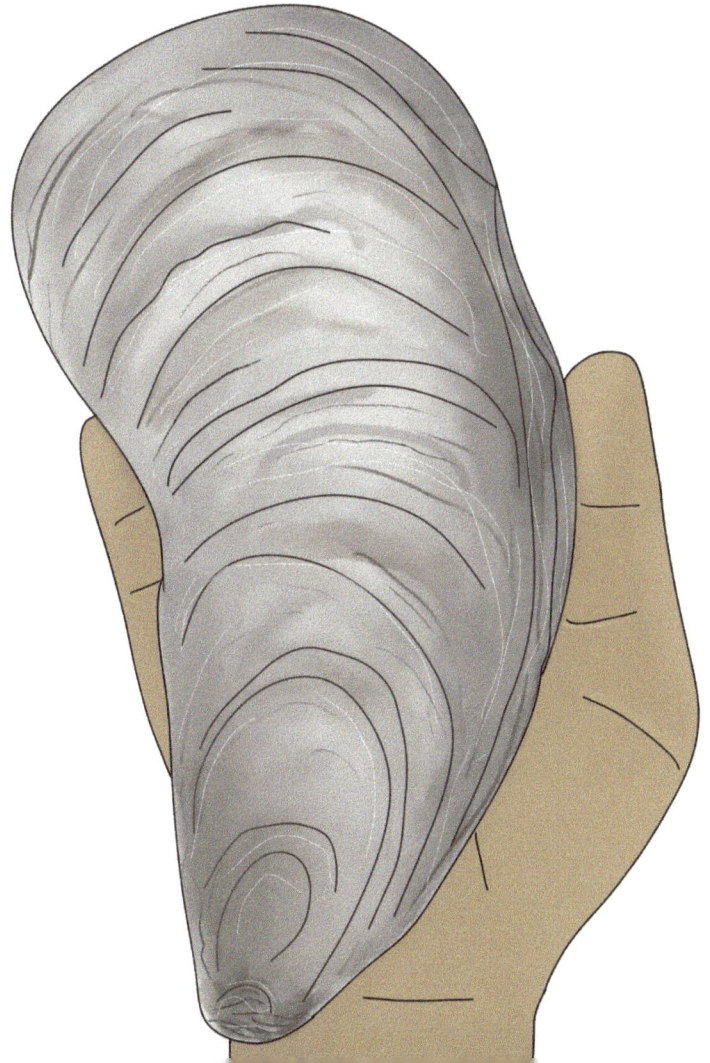

Z is for ZONE

Oysters grow in a mix of fresh and salty water. There are four zones of water in the Chesapeake Bay: tidal fresh, oligohaline (a little salty), mesohaline (salty), and polyhaline (very salty). Oysters grow in all of them but the tidal fresh zone.

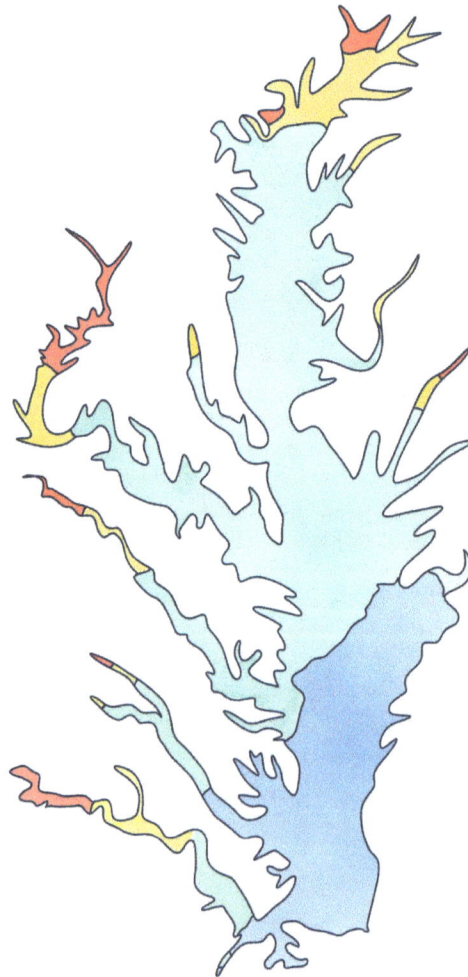

Oysters taste differently, depending on the zone or even the river they grow in! Some are very salty, some are a mix of sweet and salty, and some are not very salty at all.

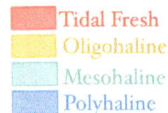

Tidal Fresh
Oligohaline
Mesohaline
Polyhaline

ACKNOWLEDGMENT

I'd like to extend a very special thank you to W.E. Kellum Seafood in Weems, Virginia, for their help and support in publishing this book. W.E. Kellum, founded by Ellery Kellum and still family-run today, has been in business since 1948 and provides oysters and scallops to many businesses all over the United States.

About the Author

Susan Swift is an accomplished teacher and elementary librarian with a lifelong passion for children's literature and a dream of writing books for kids. After graduating from the College of William and Mary, she relocated to the Northern Neck of Virginia to pursue her teaching career. Her son and her husband, a fourth-generation commercial waterman, inspired her to create her first and ongoing series, A Life of a Waterman. This series includes *The ABCs of Oystering on the Chesapeake Bay*, which follows her previous release, *The ABCs of Crabbing on the Chesapeake Bay*, published in 2024.

Susan is dedicated to educating readers of all ages about commercial fishing on the Chesapeake Bay, while presenting each book in an interesting and fun ABC format. In her personal life, Susan is the proud mother of two grown children and a son-in-law, as well as a very spoiled yellow lab. She loves spending time with her family, reading, living on the Chesapeake Bay, and visiting the Outer Banks.

About the Illustrator

Heather Cockrell has always had a passion for using her creativity to inspire children to express their own unique creativity. Heather was born and raised in the small rural town of Lancaster County, Va. After graduating from high school, Heather attended Ferrum College where she received her bachelor's degree in education. After teaching for a few years in several different areas in Virginia, Heather returned home and accepted her current position as the middle school art teacher at Northumberland Middle School in Northumberland County, Virginia. Heather finds immense joy in mentoring students, fostering their creativity, and guiding them in their artistic journeys. Her commitment extends way beyond the classroom, as she is deeply invested in many other organizations in the community. In her personal life, Heather resides in the small town of Reedville, Virginia with her husband Nick and their two dogs. She enjoys spending time on the water that both she and her husband grew up on.

www.ingramcontent.com/pod-product-compliance
Lightning Source LLC
Chambersburg PA
CBHW041426270326
41931CB00023B/3496